Crosseyed Puzzle

(Optical Illusions)

Michael John Silbaugh

Crosseyed Puzzle
Copyright © 2021 by Michael John Silbaugh

Although every precaution has been taken to verify the accuracy of the information contained herein, the author and publisher assume no responsibility for any errors or omissions. No liability is assumed for damages that may result from the use of information contained within.

ISBN-13:   Paperback: 978-1-64749-520-6
              ePub: 978-1-64749-521-3

Printed in the United States of America

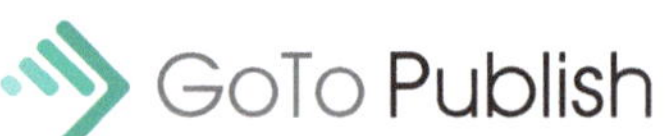

GoToPublish LLC
1-888-337-1724
www.gotopublish.com
info@gotopublish.com

To see the Optical illusions on your computer the illusion has to be 2 ½ inches wide. Zoom in or out until you get the right size.

"Crosseyed Puzzle" on plain paper use these instructions:

While looking at the center circle, slowly cross your eyes until you see two circles. This will change the Viking hats circle into the two eyes of a bison. Use these instructions on all the optical illusions.

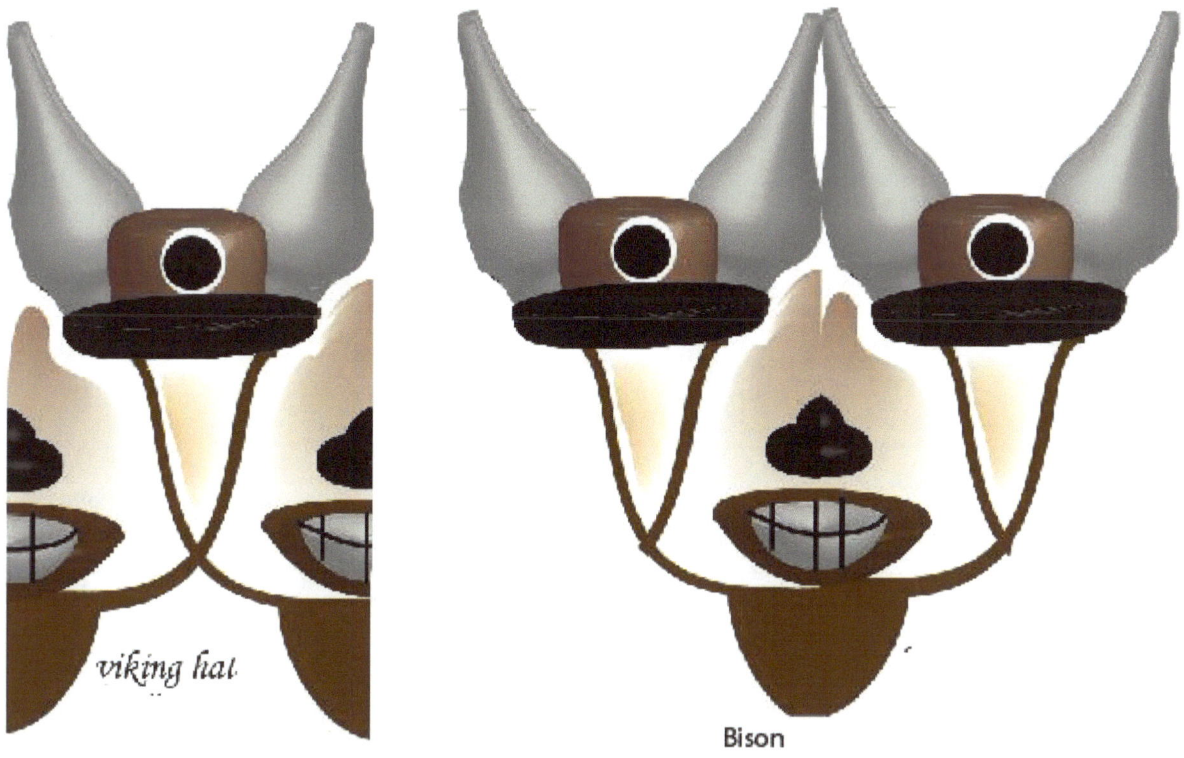

"Crosseyed Puzzle" on Transparency paper use these instructions:

Hold your index finger out and look through your finger at a back-ground. Now you should see two fingers.

Use the same instructions on the optical illusions by focusing your eyes through the transparent picture until you get a double image.

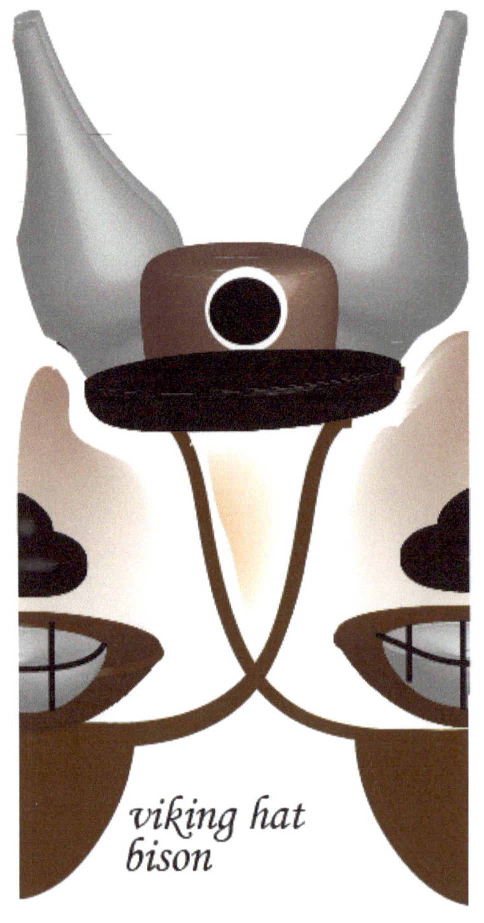

viking hat
bison

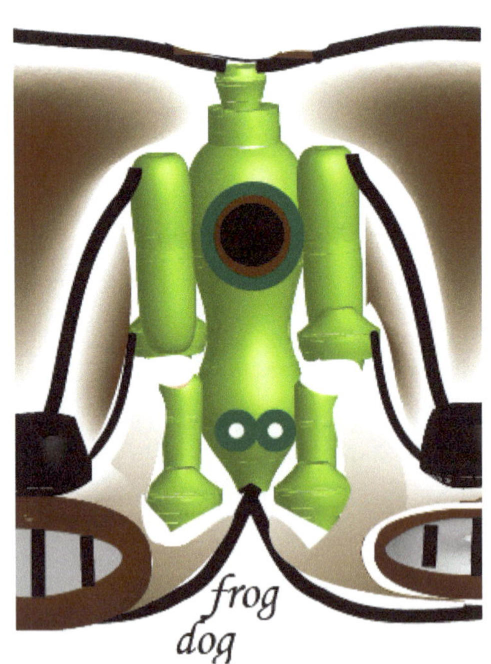

frog
dog

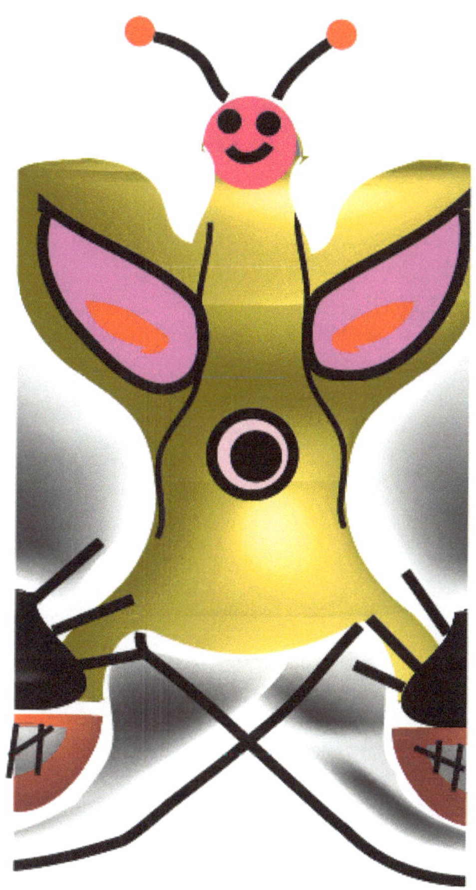

butterfly
mouse

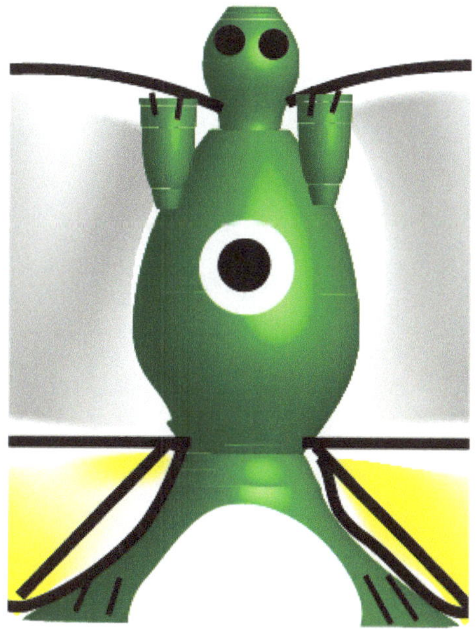

jumping frog
pinguin

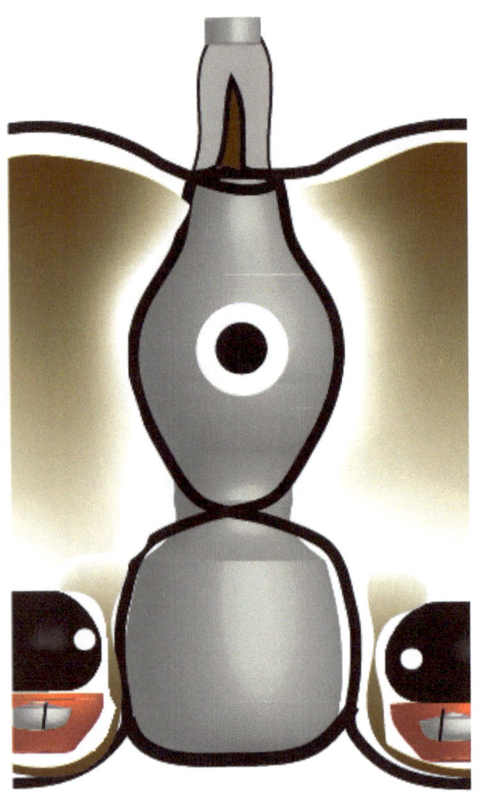

coke bottle
wolf

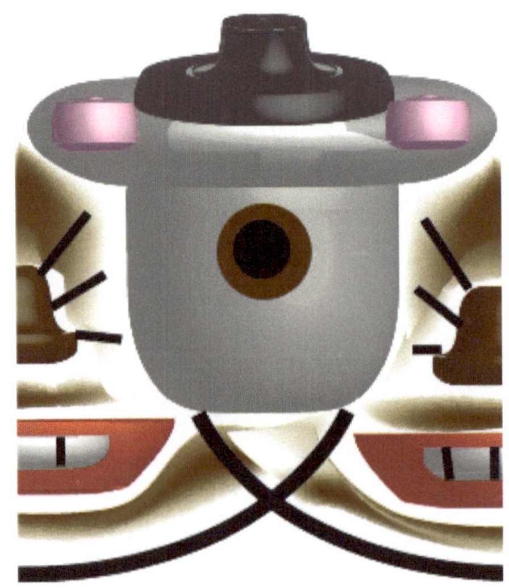

cooking pot
weasle

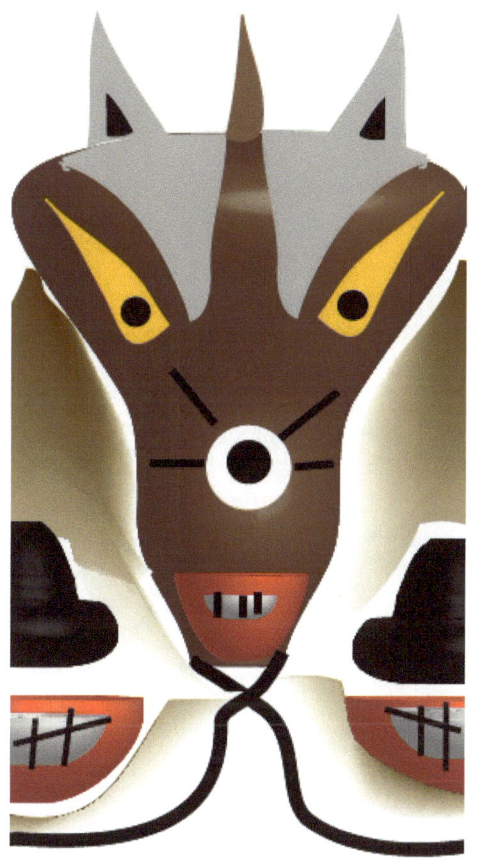

fox
gazzel

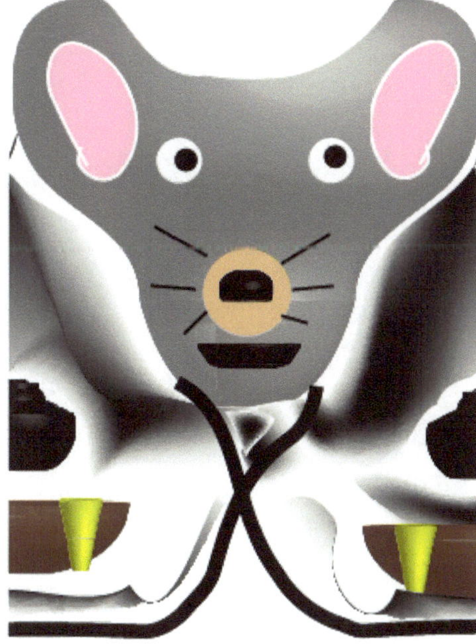

mouse
bat

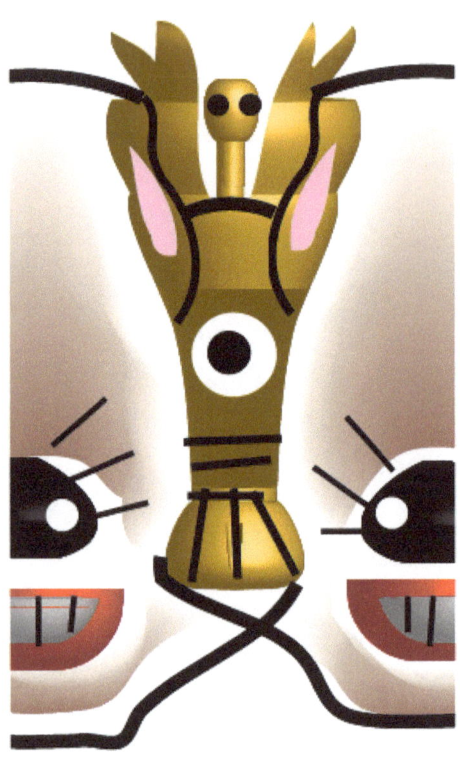

crayfish
pronghorn sheep

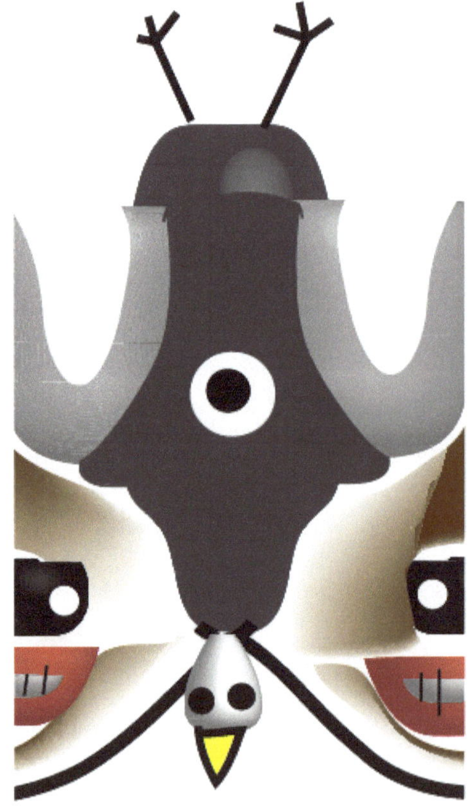

diving seagal
muskox

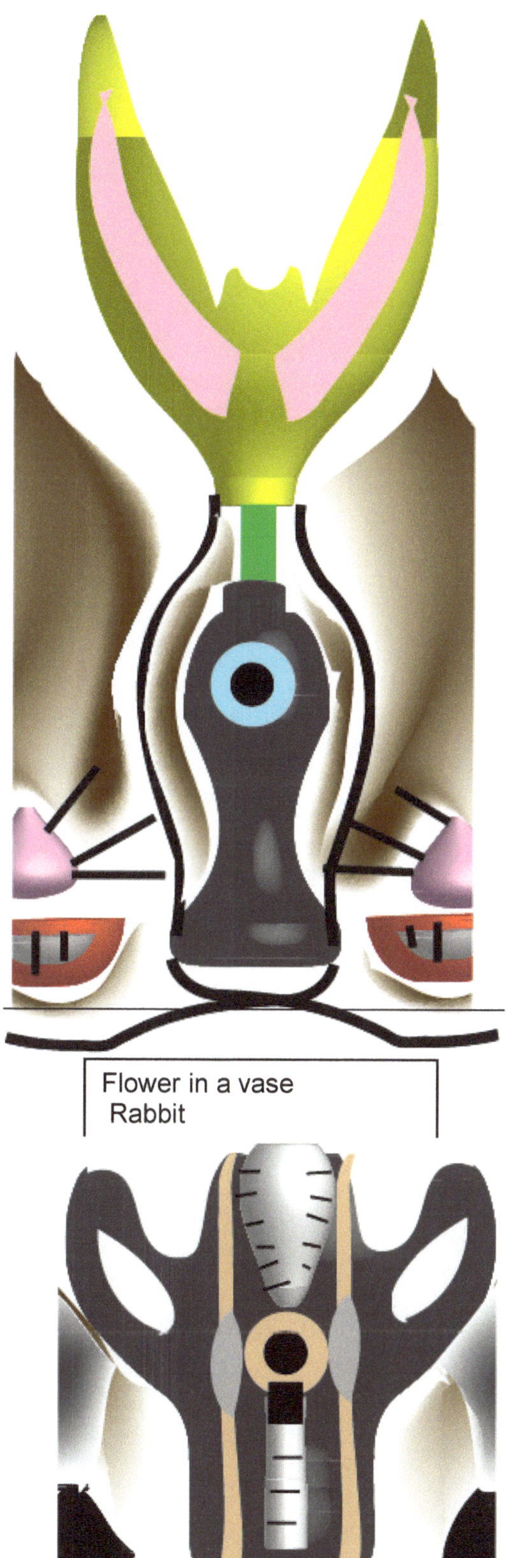

Flower in a vase
Rabbit

top view of a half zipped purse
skunk

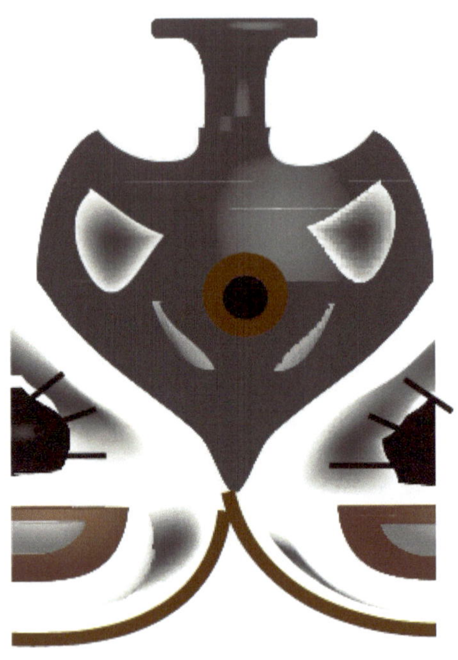

upside down spade
badger

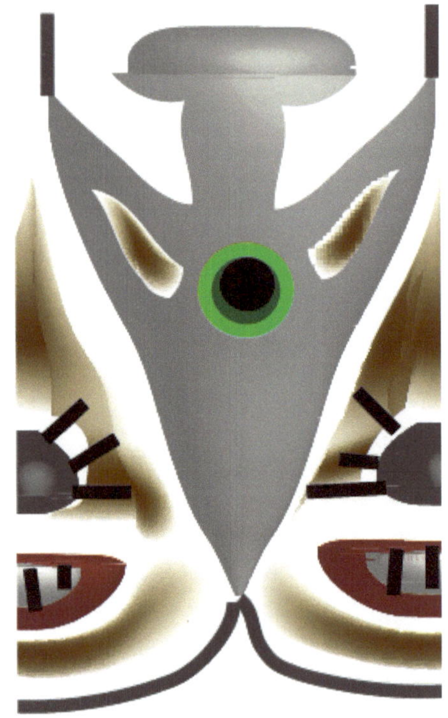

indian arrow head
linx

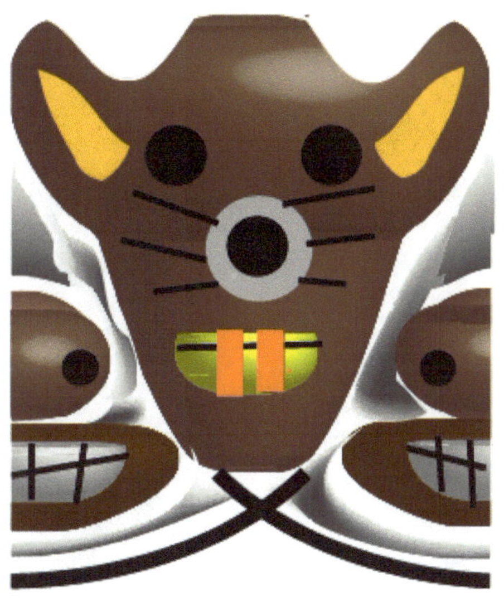

rat
monkey

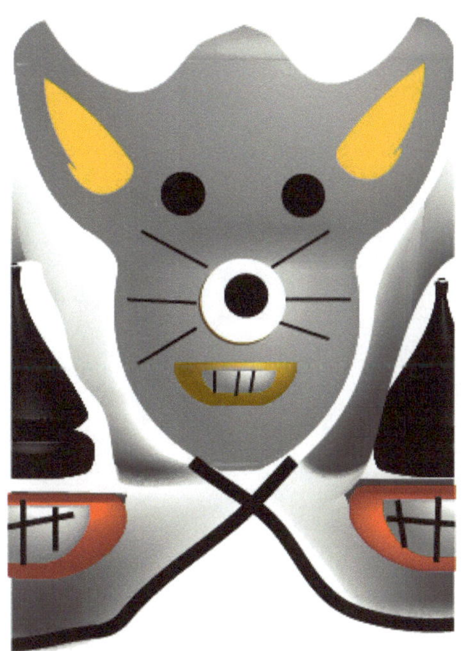

hamster
rhino

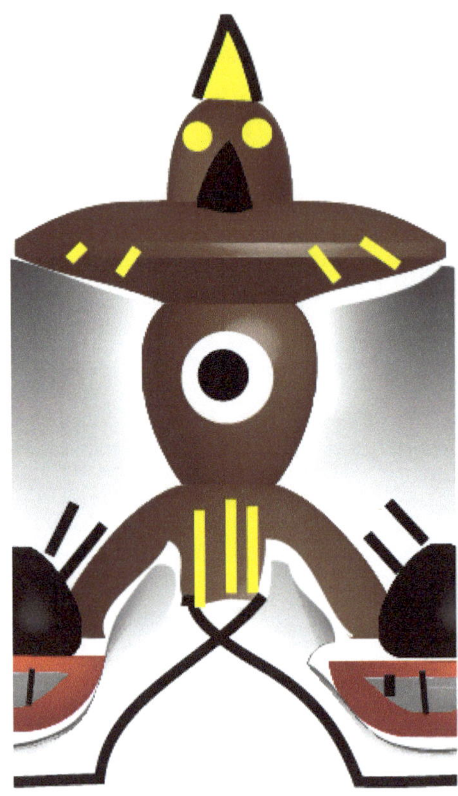

*flying bird
fox*

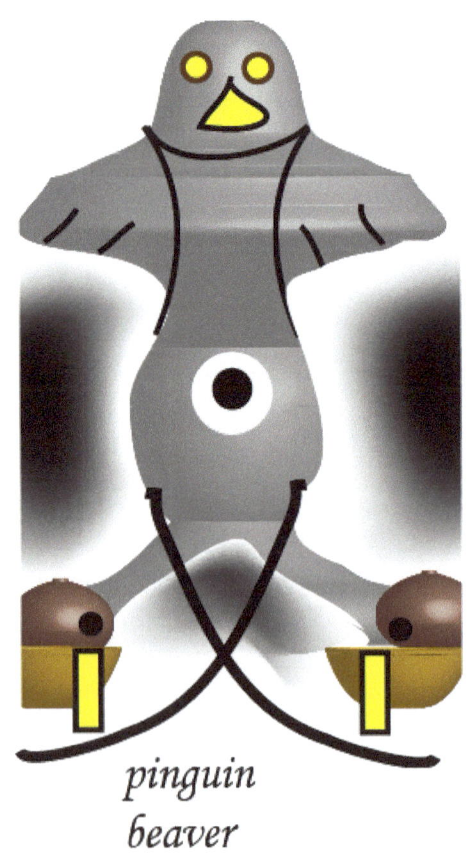

*pinguin
beaver*

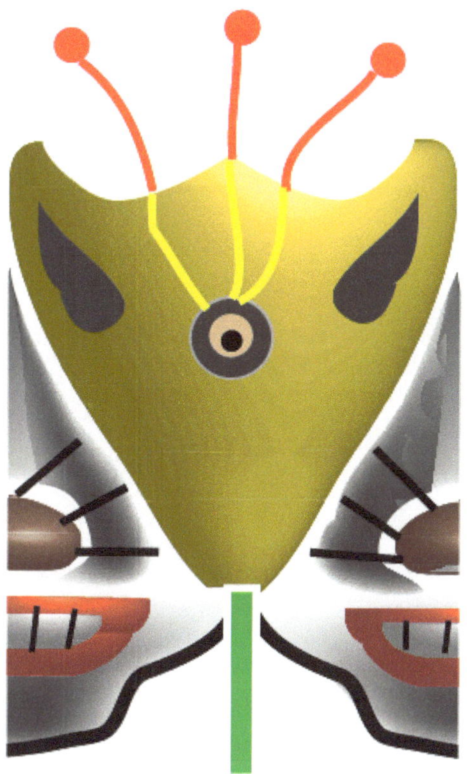

tulup
opossum

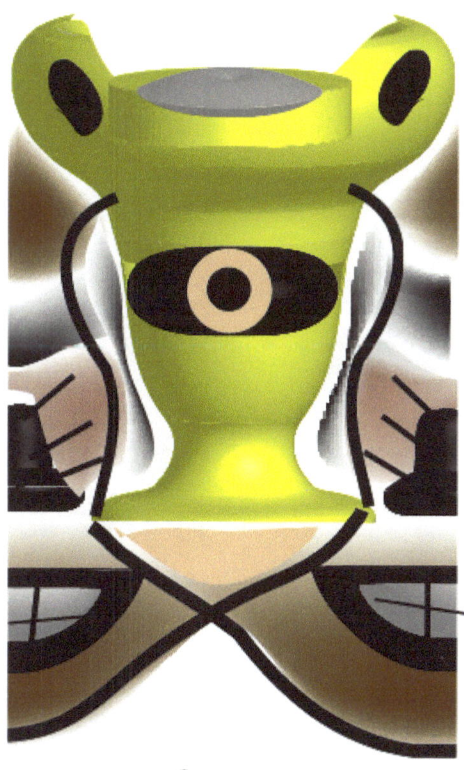

trophy
raccon

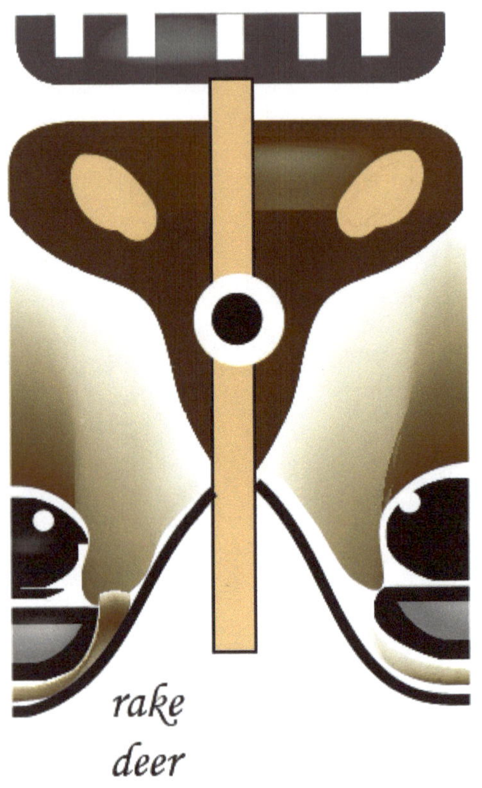

rake
deer

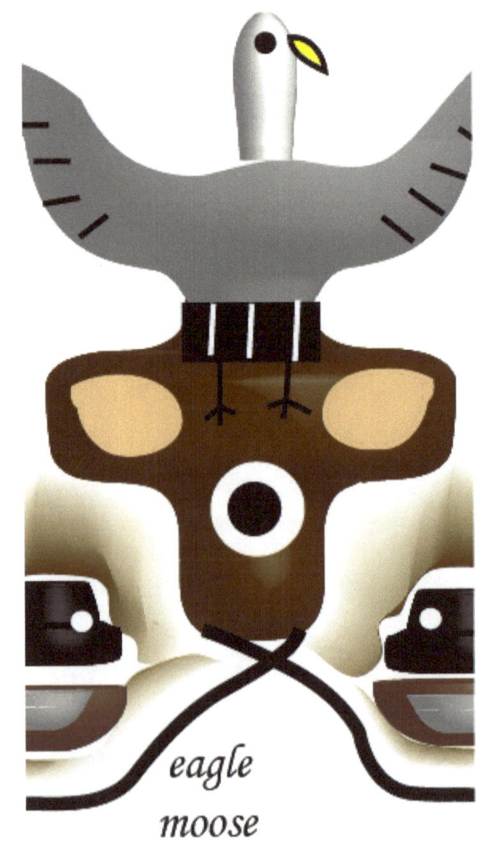

eagle
moose

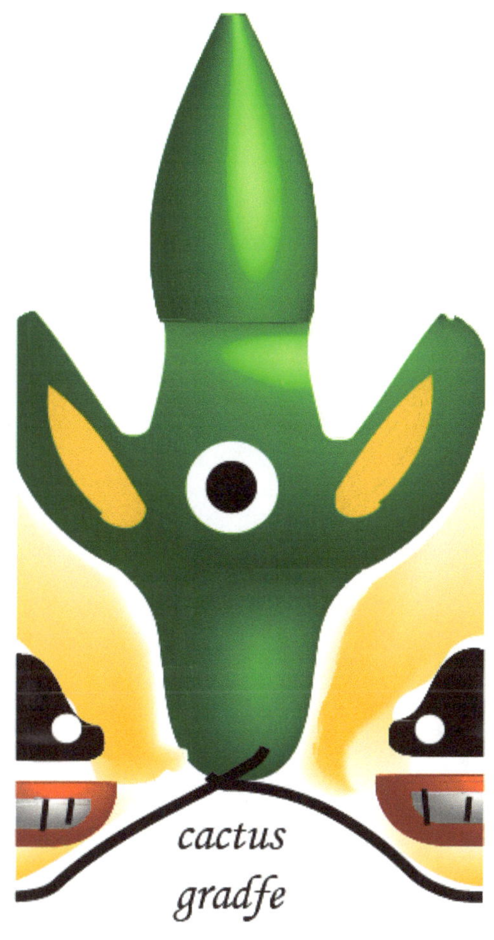

cactus
gradfe

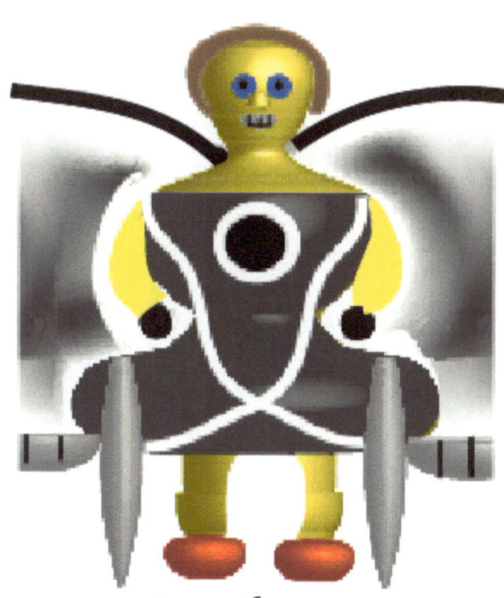

woman in a dress
walrus

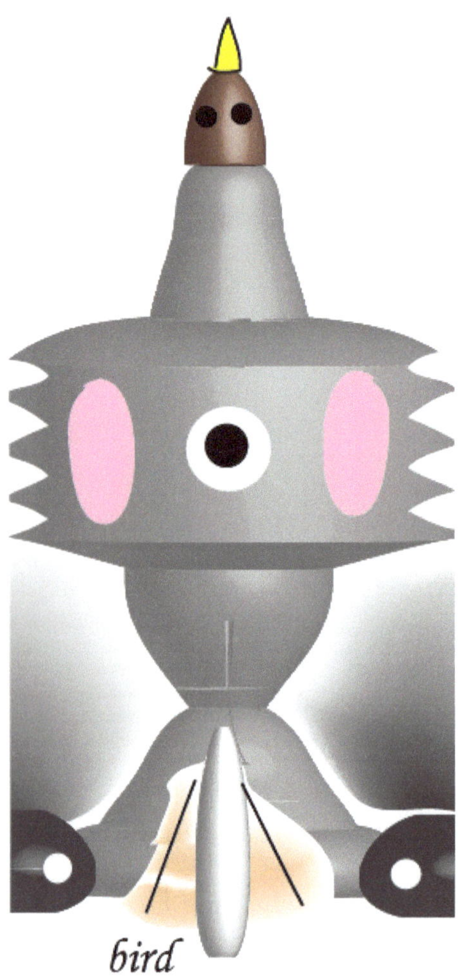

bird

elephant

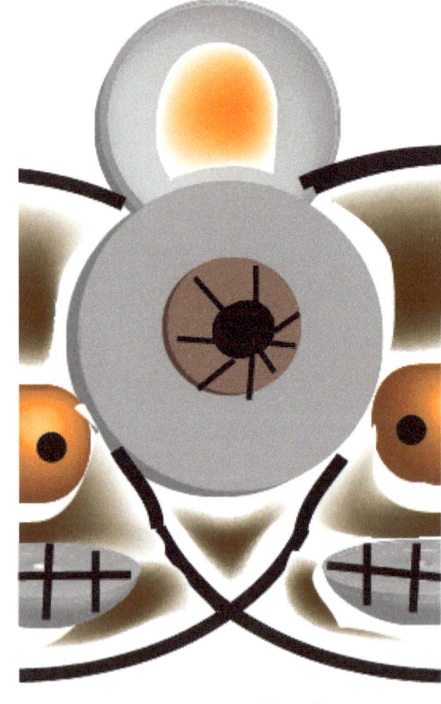

master lock

pig

heart
frog

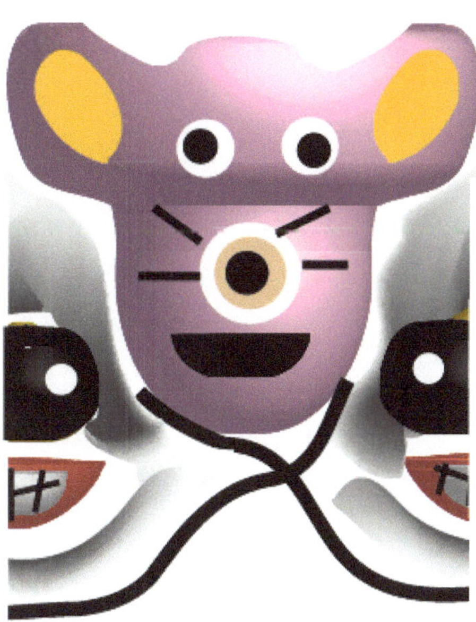

pig
panda

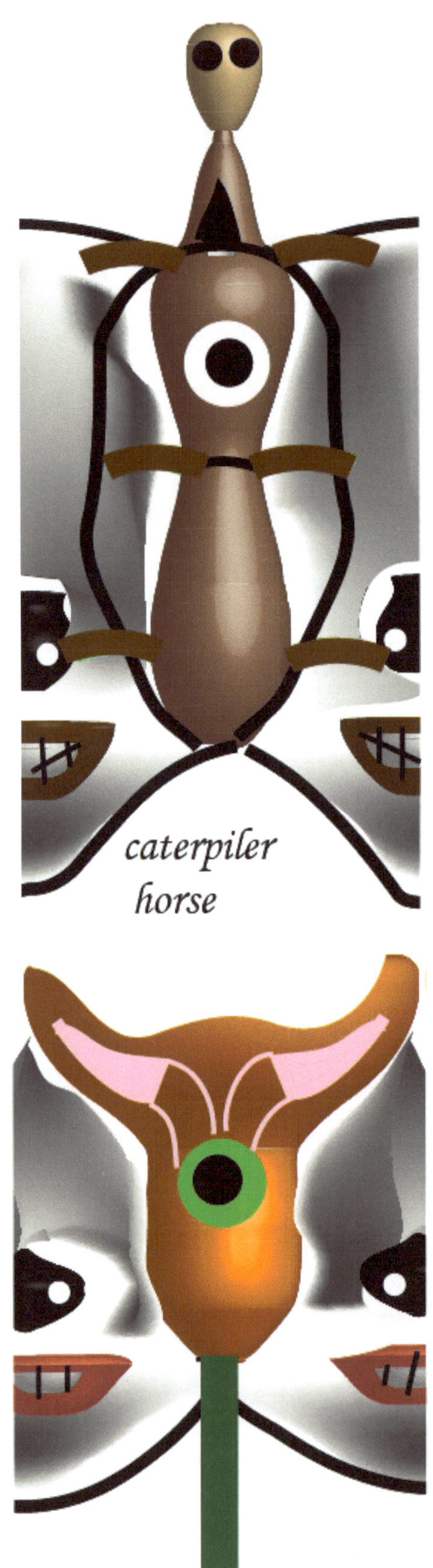
caterpiler
horse

rose
cat

www.ingramcontent.com/pod-product-compliance
Lightning Source LLC
Chambersburg PA
CBHW042146030726
47599CB00002B/632